FOREST

by Sheila Rivera

first step nonfiction

⌐ Lerner Publications Company · Minneapolis

What is a **forest?**

It is a place where many
trees and plants grow.

Not all forests are the same.

Some forests have trees with big leaves.

Some forests have lots of
evergreen trees.

It rains a lot in a
rain forest.

A forest is a kind of **habitat.**

A habitat is where plants
and animals live.

Rabbits live in the forest.

Bears live in the forest.

Frogs live in the forest too.

This deer looks for food.

A bat hangs from a tree.

Insects eat plant leaves.

Birds fly in the forest.

Many plants and animals
live in the forest.

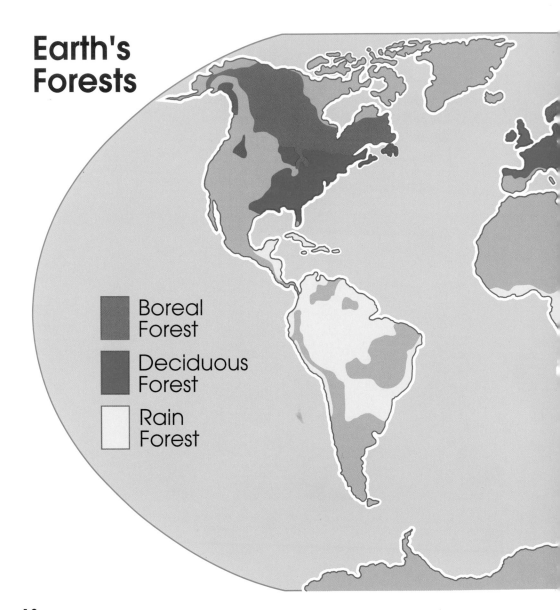

Earth's
Forests

Boreal
Forest

Deciduous
Forest

Rain
Forest

19

Forest Facts

 There are three kinds of forests: boreal forests, deciduous forests, and rain forests.

 Boreal forests have short, warm summers and long, cold, dry winters.

 Deciduous forests have four distinct seasons. In the fall, tree leaves change color.

 Rain forests have only two seasons—the rainy season and the dry season.

Some animals that live in boreal forests sleep through the winter.

 Many trees in the deciduous forest lose their leaves in the winter.

 Rain forests receive about 100 inches of rain every year. That is more than eight feet of rain!

 Birds and insects are found in every kind of forest on Earth.

Glossary

 evergreen trees – trees with leaves or needles that stay green year-round

 forest – a place where many trees grow

 habitat – where plants and animals live

 insects – animals with three body parts and six legs. Many insects have wings.

 rain forest – a thick forest that gets lots of rain

Index

The photographs in this book are reproduced through the courtesy of: © Photodisc Royalty Free by Getty Images, front cover, pp. 6, 10, 11, 12, 13, 22 (top); © James P. Rowan, pp. 2, 3, 14, 15, 22 (second from top, second from bottom); © Chad Ehlers/Photo Network, p. 4; © Carol Fuegi/CORBIS, p. 5; © Carl & Ann Purcell/CORBIS, pp. 7, 22 (bottom); © Richard Day/Daybreak Imagery, pp. 8, 22 (middle); © Tom and Pat Leeson, p. 9; © Yann Arthus-Bertrand/CORBIS, p. 16; © Kent & Donna Dannen, p. 17.

Map on pages 18–19 by Laura Westlund.

Lerner Publications Company
A division of Lerner Publishing Group
241 First Avenue North
Minneapolis, MN 55401 U.S.A.

Website address: www.lernerbooks.com

Library of Congress Cataloging-in-Publication Data

Rivera, Sheila, 1970–
        Forest / by Sheila Rivera.
            p.   cm. — (First step nonfiction)
        Includes index.
        ISBN: 0–8225–2596–8 (lib. bdg. : alk. paper)
        1. Forest animals—Juvenile literature. 2. Forest plants—Juvenile literature. I. Title.
    II. Series.
    QH86.R58 2005
    578.73—dc22   2004020788

Manufactured in the United States of America
1 2 3 4 5 6 – DP – 10 09 08 07 06 05